T0368615

Metusela Albert

NO BABY INHERITED ADAM AND EVE'S SINS.

To order additional copies of this book, contact:
Xlibris
844-714-8691
www.Xlibris.com
Orders@Xlibris.com

ISBN: Softcover   979-8-3694-3098-9
        EBook   979-8-3694-3097-2

Print information available on the last page

Rev. date: 09/26/2024

Contents

SCRIPTURE READING

Ezekiel 18:20 (King James Version).

²⁰ The soul that sinneth, it shall die. The son shall <u>not</u> bear the iniquity of the father, <u>neither</u> shall the father bear the iniquity of the son: the righteousness of the righteous shall be upon him, and the wickedness of the wicked shall be upon him.

NOTE: SIN IS <u>NOT TRANSFERABLE</u> FROM THE FATHER TO THE SON, OR FROM THE SON TO THE FATHER, OR FROM WHOSOEVER.

....
....
....

1 John 3:4 - (King James Version).

⁴ Whosoever committeth sin transgresseth also the law: for sin is the transgression of the law.

NOTE: SIN IS THE TRANSGRESSION OF GOD'S LAW.

....
....
....

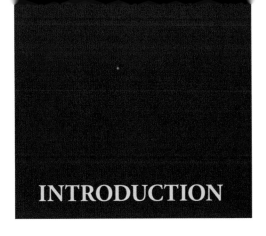

INTRODUCTION

The vast majority of Professed Christians and Mainline Denominations <u>believe and teach</u> that "BABIES ARE BORN SINNERS, DUE TO SINS <u>INHERITED</u> FROM ADAM AND EVE."

THEIR SEVEN FALSE EXPRESSIONS ABOUT SIN, ARE AS FOLLOWS:

1. We are sinners because <u>we are sinners</u>.
2. We commit sin because of Adam and Eve's sins, <u>we inherited</u>.
3. For one to be a sinner, all one must do, <u>is to be born</u>.
4. We commit sin because of <u>what we are</u>.
5. Sin is by <u>the fallen sinful nature</u>.
6. Sin is a <u>Condition</u>.
7. Sin is <u>Universal</u>, <u>due to Adam's sin in us</u>.

NOTE: THOSE SEVEN EXPRESSIONS ABOUT SIN, AS LISTED ABOVE, ARE SATANIC AND ANTI-CHRIST.

....
....
....

CHAPTER 1

THE DEFINITION OF SIN –

1 John 3:4 - (KJV). "Whosoever committeth sin transgresseth also the law: for sin is the transgression of the law."

....
....
....
....

That is the correct definition of sin. If you fail to understand the definition of Sin as given in 1 John 3:4, you are bound to have a false theory about sin, and your Salvation will be affected. Sin has to do with the transgression of GOD'S law. What law? The Ten Commandments.

GOD wrote the Ten Commandments on Two Tablets of Stone and gave through Moses on Mount Sinai when the children of Israel were delivered from slavery in Egypt. The Ten Commandments were not given for the Jews, but for all mankind. Of course, the Ten Commandments existed before the Exodus of the Jews from slavery in Egypt.

GOD'S Government in heaven where the angels existed, was ruled by law. One-third of the Angels in heaven transgressed GOD'S law. And because of their disobedience, they were cast out of heaven. They were not allowed to reside in heaven anymore.

The point stated above needs to be understood clearly by Professed Christians, that sin existed in heaven, and God's Government was ruled by law.

In heaven, the angels did <u>not</u> have a fallen sinful nature, yet they committed sin. Therefore, <u>sin cannot be defined by the fallen sinful nature</u>. Period.

NOTE: Sin has to do with the transgression of GOD'S law. Yeah! . . . GOD'S law existed in heaven, though <u>not</u> in written form like it was written on two Tablets of Stone, at MOUNT SINAI.

....
....
....

COMMANDMENT # 1, GOD says, "Thou shalt have no other gods before <u>me</u>."

....
....
....

Commandment # 1 is a <u>Universal law</u> because worship is due only to the Creator.

When the angel, Lucifer, coveted <u>to be like GOD</u>, <u>that was a transgression of GOD'S law.</u> (Isaiah 14:12-14).

Remember this: GOD will forgive genuinely repentant sinners and welcome them to heaven. (Luke 15:7, 10). If Lucifer and one-third of the angels genuinely repented in heaven, GOD could have forgiven them, and perhaps not cast them out.

A HIGH POINT TO ALWAYS REMEMBER: The angels in heaven did <u>not</u> have a fallen sinful nature yet committed sin. Therefore, the idea that says, Sin is by nature, is <u>not</u> correct and must be corrected, condemned, and rebuked.

Furthermore, Adam and Eve sinned without a fallen sinful nature. Therefore, Sin <u>cannot</u> be defined by the sinful nature, but by the transgression of GOD'S law.

THE FALLEN SINFUL NATURE WAS <u>THE RESULT OF SIN, NOT THE CAUSE OF SIN.</u>

UNDERSTAND THIS: THE RESULT OF SIN, AND THE CAUSE OF SIN, ARE TWO DIFFERENT THINGS.

//
//
//

Unfortunately, most Professed Christians do <u>not</u> understand the simple difference. Yes, they don't get it; and that is the reason they continue to believe that <u>Babies Are Born Sinners</u>. They lost their reasoning power. And sin becomes excusable. Thus, GOD becomes responsible for sin since He created us. That is why we have to confront, condemn, and rebuke, that SATANIC, ANTI-CHRIST doctrine.

....
....
....

We must continue to maintain a strong reasoning power to learn to differentiate things. And if we did not reason well, try and listen to other views presented by others, have an open mind, and a humble spirit. Thus, GOD will direct us to the truth as presented by others.

....
....
....

When people don't understand the cause of sin, hence, their understanding of How to be forgiven is also distorted. And How to be Saved, is also affected.

This saying is so true. Wide is the road that leads to Destruction, and so many people go through it. Narrow is the path that leads to Salvation, and only a few walk enter.

GOD, please have mercy upon us, and help us to remember your love to forgive us when we come in faith and repentance. Thank you.

....
....
....

Dear Reader,

DO YOU KNOW THE DIFFERENCE?

THE TRUTH	THE ERROR
• SIN IS THE TRANSGRESSION OF GOD'S LAW. • 1 John 3:4. • NOTE: YOU ARE RESPONSIBLE FOR YOUR CHOICE.	• SIN IS BY THE FALLEN SINFUL NATURE. • .... • This definition blames God for creating you a sinner without your choice. • According to this definition, sin is inherited.

Compiled by: Metusela F. Albert

Dear friends, Don't buy the lie of the mainline Denominations that advocate – Sin Is Inherited / Babies Are Born Sinners.

THE TRUTH IS: BABIES ARE <u>NOT</u> BORN SINNERS. . . . GOD CREATED <u>NO</u> BABY SINNERS.

If you need more information, try and acquire these <u>two Books</u> and read for your understanding.

PUBLISHED ON MARCH 04, 2011

PUBLISHED ON JUNE 01, 2021

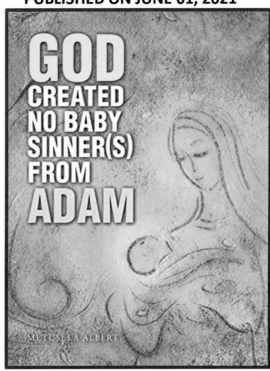

....
....
....

CHAPTER 2

NO BABY WAS BORN A MURDERER.

If you believe that Babies Are Born Sinners, then you would also have to believe that Babies Are Born Murderers. Therefore, you would have to admit that God was the One that Created every murderer. Thus, you would have to accept that King David was not at fault for murdering Uriah, the husband of Bathsheba. Are you willing to justify King David for killing Uriah?. . . . Are you??? . . . And you would have to accept all criminals who killed people in the community as not guilty. Are you willing to go that direction?

HERE IS THE THING. . . . No sound minded person would believe that a killer is justified for killing his or her neighbor by such reasoning that God is at fault for creating a person a killer / a murderer.

It is time that we stand up for JESUS, confront, rebuke, and condemn such heretical teachings in the CHURCHES. In fact, the Churches are the agent of the Devil in promoting such evil doctrines to prevail in Christianity.

PUBLISHED ON MARCH 04, 2011

PUBLISHED ON JUNE 01, 2021

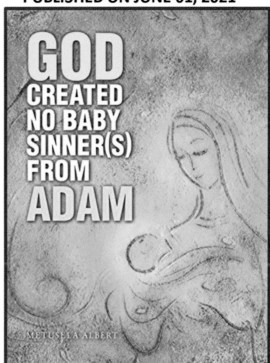

....

....

....

CHAPTER 3

NO BABY WAS BORN A ROBBER / A THIEF.

Let's get it right. GOD did <u>not</u> create one baby in the mother's womb, a robber / a thief.

Very often we see on the news the numerous break-ins to the shops. If we believed in Babies Are Born Sinners, Born Robbers, therefore, we would have to admit that those who steal are not criminals and should be acquitted; for they are innocent. Thus, we should admit that GOD is to be blamed for creating baby robbers in the mother's womb.

This Devilish doctrine called – "<u>Babies Are Born Sinners</u>" should be condemned by sound minded Christians. Instead, Christianity is promoting evil doctrines that increases lawlessness in the community and Churches. Sad.

I wrote two Books as shown below, to deal with the false subject called – "BABIES ARE BORN SINNERS." But that seems to be not enough since this false belief about "Babies Are Born Sinners" is becoming the norm of today. Therefore, I had to write another Book, to provoke Professed Christians to think and reason like a mature person.

That belief justifies sin and makes GOD become responsible for sin. What a shame. I can understand if a Professed Christian commits sin. But for the Church to advocate a doctrine that justifies sin, and makes GOD become responsible for lawlessness, I don't understand; and it is not acceptable. I am yelling in here for Christianity to wake up and stop blaming and promoting GOD for lawlessness in the society.

PUBLISHED ON MARCH 04, 2011

PUBLISHED ON JUNE 01, 2021

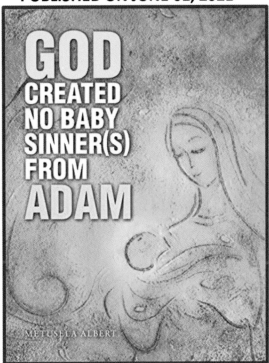

NOTE: The Seventh-day Adventist Church claims to be GOD'S ONLY REMNANT CHURCH that has the truth, yet still believes in the false doctrine called – "BABIES ARE BORN SINNERS."

Their written materials testify to it. It is one of the doctrines documented in their 28 Fundamental Beliefs Book. Sad to say, the world is converting the Church, the Pastors, including the members.

Other mega / mainstream Churches believe in that false teaching. Go online and check it out for yourself.

....

....

....

CHAPTER 4

KING DAVID WAS <u>NOT</u> BORN A MURDERER.

King David made a choice to commit adultery with Bathsheba, the wife of Uriah. When Bathsheba became pregnant, David tried to cover up his sin and went too far and committed a murder plan against Uriah, the husband of Bathsheba. This is unacceptable. God was displeased with David.

Later, King David realized his evil habit, and genuinely repented as recorded in Psalm 51 and 32. God forgave King David for admitting and confessing his sin.

What is the Point? God did not create King David a murderer or an adulterer. It was King David who made the choice to commit sin. He is responsible for the sins committed. God is not responsible for the sins committed by King David.

Dear folks, this subject must be understood well, otherwise, Sin is excused in the Churches because of the false teachings of the Churches.

PUBLISHED ON MARCH 04, 2011

PUBLISHED ON JUNE 01, 2021

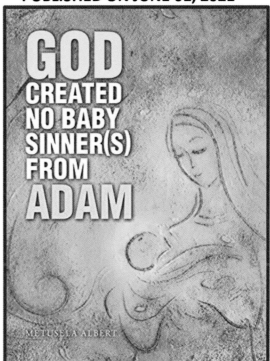

....
....
....

CHAPTER 5

BATHSHEBA WAS NOT BORN AN ADULTERER.

Bathsheba, the wife of Uriah, committed adultery with King David by her own choice. She did not commit adultery without her choice. Sin is the transgression of God's law. In the Ten Commandments, there is a law that says, thou shalt not commit adultery.

She did not commit adultery due to her fallen sinful nature inherited from Adam and Eve.

Dear folks, let's make sure this subject about sin is clear. NO BABY INHERITED SIN FROM ADAM AND EVE.

PUBLISHED ON MARCH 04, 2011

PUBLISHED ON JUNE 01, 2021

CHAPTER 6

RAHAB AND MARY MAGDALENE WERE NOT BORN PROSTITUTES.

When the children of Israel crossed River Jordan to Canaan, the Promised Land, GOD instructed Joshua to take the children of Israel and walk round the city Jericho once a day for six days and return to base. On the seventh day, they were to walk around the city one more time, and at the end of their walk, blow the trumpets and shout; and the city is to be destroyed. Rahab, who was a prostitute, hid the two Israelite spies in her home. She believed in the GOD of the children of Israel. Eventually, she and her household were saved. She was not born a Prostitute. She made that bad decision by her choice. Therefore, the belief that says, Babies Are Born Sinners, is not correct and needs to be corrected, condemned, and rebuked.

Mary Magdalene, the sister of Lazarus whom JESUS resurrected after four days in the tomb, was **not** born a Prostitute. She also made a bad decision. But she later repented and was forgiven by JESUS. While she was an active Prostitute, she was **not** forgiven of her sin. Only when she <u>genuinely repented of sin,</u> then the gift of forgiveness and Salvation was granted to her.

WE ARE <u>NOT</u> BORN SINNERS. NO BABY WAS BORN A PROSTITUTE.

”””
”””
”””

CHAPTER 7

NO BABY WAS BORN AN IDOL WORSHIPPER.

The second commandment in the Ten Commandments tells us not to worship idols. Imagine, if you believe that Babies Are Born Sinners, hence, you will have to admit that it was God who created Baby Idol Worshipers, in the mother's womb.

You may recall the time when Moses and Joshua were communing with GOD at Mount Horeb, and the children of Israel were at the foot of the Mount were worshipping an idol, led by Aaron, the brother of Moses. GOD was displeased with them and had to destroy about 3,000 people.

These people would be innocent "IF" Babies Are Born Sinners, Born Idol Worshippers. Of course, and GOD would not have destroyed them neither their idol god.

....
....
....

WHAT IS THE POINT?

The belief that says, Babies Are Born Sinners because we inherited Adam and Eve's sins, is SATANIC and LAWLESS. We must stand up against that Devilish doctrine. We must confront it, condemn it, and rebuke it.

I wrote this Book to condemn it. And the Churches that teach that Devilish doctrine should be condemned without sparing the rod.

Dear folks, don't be afraid to stand up against your Denomination, if your Church is advocating that evil doctrine that says, Babies Are Born Sinners, Sin Is by Nature, We Inherited Adam and Eve's Sins, We Are Sinners Because We Are Sinners, etc.

....
....
....

PUBLISHED ON MARCH 04, 2011

PUBLISHED ON JUNE 01, 2021

....
....
....

Let me remind us again of the Seven False Expressions about Sin. Whenever you hear of those expression, you should be able to recognize the SATANIC teaching that infiltrated the Christian Churches. You need to confront it, rebuke it, and condemn it harshly.

Don't allow the Devil to lie about our only GOD who loved us and created us in his image.

SEVEN <u>FALSE</u> EXPRESSIONS ABOUT SIN - BY THOSE WHO TEACH

"BABIES ARE BORN SINNERS" :

1. We are sinners because we are sinners.
2. We commit sin because of Adam's sin we inherited.
3. For one to be a sinner, all one must do, is to be born.
4. We commit sin because of what we are.
5. Sin is by the fallen sinful nature.
6. Sin is a Condition.
7. Sin is universal due to Adam's sin in us.

DEVILISH

DEVILISH

Compiled by: Metusela F. Albert.

Once again, thank you for standing up to uphold the truth about <u>JESUS, our only GOD,</u> who loved us and <u>created us in His image</u>. HE is sitting on the THRONE, in heaven.

Thank you for sharing this truth with your friends.

....
....
....

CHAPTER 8

THE DIFFERENCE BETWEEN <u>THE FIRST DEATH</u> AND <u>THE SECOND DEATH</u>.

After Adam and Eve sinned, they died the first death after living some years. They lost immortality and became mortal. Had they died eternally, they would have had <u>no opportunity</u> of repenting of their sins and be forgiven by God.

In Genesis 2:16-17, when God told them that the day they eat of the forbidden fruit, they would surely die; that death was not intended to be eternal death, but a temporary death called – a sleep. This death is called the FIRST DEATH.

<u>WHAT THREE THINGS</u> WE INHERITED FROM ADAM AND EVE???

1. We inherited <u>the FIRST DEATH</u>.
2. We inherited <u>a MORTAL BODY</u>.
3. We inherited <u>a SINFUL NATURE</u>.

WHAT FOUR THINGS WE DID NOT INHERIT FROM ADAM AND EVE???

1. We did not inherit Sin.
2. We did not inherit a Sinless Nature.
3. We did not inherit the Second Death which is Eternal Death.
4. We did not inherit the IMMORTAL BODY.

NOTE: JESUS inherited those four things listed above when He became human flesh through Mary at Bethlehem.

The Eternal Death is also called the Second Death which will take place at the end of the Millennium. Eternal Death is the wages of Sin (Romans 6:23). Eternal Death is the Death mentioned in Ezekiel 18:20. It is not transferable from the father to the son or from the son to the father.

BOTTOM-LINE IS: NO BABY INHERITED ADAM AND EVE'S SINS. BABIES ARE NOT BORN SINNERS.

....
....
....

CHAPTER 9

JESUS WAS BORN WITH THE FALLEN SINFUL NATURE, LIKE ALL BABIES.

Because JESUS was born with the fallen sinful nature like us, He was tempted in all things as we are yet sinned not. HE was mortal, subject to the first death. The Roman soldiers tortured and killed him on the Cross at Calvary. They killed only His human Mortal Body, not His Divine Nature.

A CRUCIAL POINT: If JESUS was born without a fallen sinful nature and without a mortal body like us, then He could not have become our example in how to live holy. He kept the law holy to show us that the law can be kept holy, when He abides in us.

....
....
....

CHAPTER 10

ETERNAL DEATH WILL TAKE PLACE AFTER THE MILLENNIUM (1,000 years).

At the second Coming of JESUS, the righteous, dead and alive, will be taken to heaven. The 144,000 mentioned in the Book of Revelation Chapter 7, are the righteous that are alive. They will be translated and taken to heaven. They will not experience the first death. I wrote a Book - The 144,000 in the Book of Revelation. It is a literal number.

The second coming of JESUS marks the beginning of the Millennium (1,000 years). At the end of the Millennium, JESUS comes back the third time. The wicked will be resurrected at this time. This is called the Second Resurrection. Only the wicked will be resurrected at the third coming of JESUS. And this Resurrection is called the Second Resurrection.

Blessed are they that are resurrected in the first Resurrection – (Revelation 20:5-6).

And the New Jerusalem city comes down with JESUS. And fire comes down to destroy the wicked including Satan and

his angels. After that, the earth will be renewed. And the righteous will dwell with GOD on this new earth.

....
....
....

CHAPTER 11

NO ONE WILL BE JUDGED BY THE FALLEN SINFUL NATURE.

We will all be judged by the law of GOD. Read Ecclesiastes 12:13-14 – (King James Version).

v13. Let us hear the conclusion of the whole matter: Fear God, and keep his commandments: for this is the whole duty of man.

v14. For God shall bring every work into judgment, with every secret thing, whether it be good, or whether it be evil.

....
....
....

We inherited <u>the Fallen Sinful Nature</u> from Adam and Eve. And sin is <u>not</u> by the Fallen Sinful Nature. Sin is a choice, <u>not</u> by inheritance.

....
....
....

NOTE: Your Fallen Sinful Nature is <u>not</u> going to stop you from going to heaven. It is your transgression of GOD'S law that will stop you from entering heaven, <u>if you do not confess and repent of your sins committed by your choice.</u> You are responsible for your sins committed by your own choice. GOD is not responsible for sin. HE will not condemn you for your fallen sinful nature. But you will be condemned for committing sin by your own choice.

///
///
///

Sin has to do with the transgression of GOD'S law, not with the fallen sinful nature. Have you ever heard anyone praying and saying, "GOD, please forgive me for my fallen sinful nature." . . . Have you heard? No? Why? Because, no person was Born a Sinner, due to the fallen sinful nature, inherited.

....
....
....

Dear folks, stop being fooled by others and the mainline Denominations for telling you – WE ARE BORN SINNERS.

....
....
....

Here is a crucial point that most people who believe in <u>Babies Are Born Sinners,</u> failed to understand.

WHAT IS THE CRUCIAL POINT?

If we will be judged by the Fallen Sinful Nature, then it makes sense to define Sin by the Fallen Sinful Nature. Then it would make sense to believe that Babies Are Born Sinners. But since we will be judged by the law, therefore, Babies Are <u>NOT</u> Born Sinners. It is so simple, yet most people still have not able to reason logically and biblically.

WHY SO MANY MAINLINE DENOMINATIONS STILL HAVE <u>NOT</u> UNDERSTOOD IT?

Read Ecclesiastes 12:13-14. Further reading – 1 John 3:4 and Ezekiel 18:20.

We as Professed Christians must stand up against the False Teaching that is - ANTI-CHRIST.

....

....

....

CHAPTER 12

EVERYONE WILL BE JUDGED BY THE TEN COMMANDMENTS.

There are three key Scriptures to help us understand this subject well. Ezekiel 18:20; 1 John 3:4; and Ecclesiastes 12:13-14.

LET'S READ - Ecclesiastes 12:13-14. (King James Version).

v.13. Let us hear the conclusion of the whole matter: **Fear God, and keep his commandments: for this is the whole duty of man**.

v.14. **For God shall bring every work into judgment, with every secret thing, whether it be good, or whether it be evil.**

The text above is self-explanatory. Everyone that was born to this earth will be judged by GOD'S law.

What about the Baby that died at an early age; for example, a baby that died during delivery time by the mother, and the baby that died at an age that is very young? What Sin they committed? None.

We must leave the unknown with GOD who knows everyone's future. GOD already knew the kind of life the baby would grow up and live as an adult person, before the baby was born. Think of yourself. GOD knew your future lifestyle before you were even born. Allow GOD to be the judge who knows everyone. The point is – We will all be judged by the Ten Commandments. Sin is no excuse. Thus, NO Baby was Born a Sinner. NO Baby was a Sinner by the Fallen Sinful Nature. NO baby inherited Adam and Eve's sins. Period!

TAKE CARE AND GOD BLESS.

....
....
....

NOTE: Understanding the Scripture above will lead one to realize that the Belief that says, "Babies Are Born Sinners due to Adam and Eve's sins," is incorrect and Satanic. It is so simple.

Unfortunately, most people rely on their Churches to tell them of the truth, instead of reading the Scriptures and asking GOD to show them the truth. Hence, the Churches brainwashed them.

Dear folks, this is 2024. We need to think for ourselves and seek GOD earnestly, to reveal the truth. When we seek GOD for guidance to find the truth, we will find.

In Matthew 7:7, JESUS said, Ask and ye shall receive. Seek and he shall find. Knock and the door shall be opened.

Listen to other views but do your own evaluation as to which is the truth.

Thank you for reading this Book. I hope your reading of this Book is by God's leading to find the truth that has been hidden for so many years.

....
....
....

CONCLUSION.

<u>No Baby Inherited the Sins of Adam and Eve.</u> Cain and Abel did <u>not</u> inherit the sins of their parents. Of course, Babies Are <u>NOT</u> Born Sinners.

Our GOD who loved us created no Baby sinners from Adam and Eve's sins. GOD created all Babies in His image, <u>not</u> in the Devil's image, a sinner.

When you know the truth, you will easily know the error(s). But if you don't know the truth, you will not know the error(s). Since you have known the truth, it is your responsibility to share with others, to help them not to believe again in that false teaching that says, Babies Are Born Sinners.

Give GOD the Glory, Honor, and Praise.

Wishing you and your family much of GOD'S mercies and good health.

....
....
....

Feel free to contact me, should you need to speak personally with me. My email address: **metusela_albert@yahoo.com**

I would love to hear from you. Thank you.

....
....
....

- THE END -

Printed in the United States
by Baker & Taylor Publisher Services

* * *

Metusela F. Albert says, "When you know the truth, you will easily know the error(s). But if you don't know the truth, you will not know the error(s)."

* * *

This book is going to blow your mind with exclusive truth that has been hidden for decades because it was not understood by the mainline Christian (Protestant) Churches and denominations.

Read it for yourself and stop being deceived by your own church. You are going to learn something that you had not known before about JESUS in the Old and New Testaments; and his two natures during his incarnation on earth.

Did you not know yet that the Almighty God of Abraham did not have a Son in heaven called Jesus? . . . Did you? . . . Really?

Of course! JESUS was the Almighty God of Abraham before his incarnation through Mary at Bethlehem. HE alone created the heaven and the earth. There is no other God besides him. None before him and after him.

Worship is due to JESUS alone. He was the Father who became the Son of God through Mary at Bethlehem by the incarnation process.

While JEHOVAH was in human flesh called Jesus, he did not cease from being God the Father. As an immortal God from eternity, Jesus Christ's divinity cannot die. Therefore, only his humanity died at Calvary.

ISBN 979-8-3694-3098-9

51499

Xlibris

METUSELA ALBERT

WHO IS SITTING ON THE
THRONE, IN HEAVEN?
JESUS, THE ONLY GOD.